Sea Turtles

Victoria Blakemore

For Trish, for always making me laugh. By the way, have you seen my stapler?

© 2017 Victoria Blakemore

All rights reserved. This book or parts thereof may not be reproduced in any form, stored in any retrieval system, or transmitted in any form by any means—electronic, mechanical, photocopy, recording, or otherwise—without prior written permission of the publisher, except as provided by United States of America copyright law. For permission requests, write to the publisher, at "Attention: Permissions Coordinator," at the address below.

vblakemore.author@gmail.com

Copyright info/picture credits

Cover, Shane Myers Photography/Shutterstock; Page 3, Pexels/Pixabay; Page 5, 12019/Pixabay; Page 7, Pexels/Pixabay; Page 9, Pexels/Pixabay; Pages 10-11, rawenergy/Pixabay; Page 13, Richard Carey/AdobeStock; Page 15, kracmar/Pixabay; Page 17, DanniePhoto/Pixabay; Page 19, dkatana/Pixabay; Page 21, skeeze/Pixabay; Page 23; taylorkleklamp/Pixabay; Page 25, Felix_Broennimann/Pixabay; Page 27, Pexels/Pixabay; Page 29, dimitrisvetsikas1969/Pixabay; Page 31, sarangib/Pixabay; Page 33, Shane Myers Photography/Shutterstock

Table of Contents

What are Sea Turtles?	2
Size	4
Physical Characteristics	6
Habitat	8
Range	10
Diet	12
Communication	16
Movement	18
Young Sea Turtles	20
Sea Turtle Life	22
Lifespan	24
Population	26
Sea Turtles in Danger	28
Helping Sea Turtles	30
Glossary	34

What Are Sea Turtles?

Sea turtles are reptiles. They are **cold-blooded** animals. They are related to other turtles and tortoises.

There are eight different kinds of sea turtles. They differ in size, color, where they live, and what they eat.

Sea turtles can be yellow, brown, black, or green in color. They can be many different shades of green.

Size

Sea turtles range in size from about two feet long to over six feet long. They often weigh between sixty and 200 pounds.

The leatherback sea turtle is the largest kind of sea turtle. They can grow to be over six feet long and weigh over 1,000 pounds.

Male and female sea turtles are usually about the same size.

Physical Characteristics

Sea turtles are known for their hard shell. It protects them from predators. Most sea turtles have hard plates called **scutes** on their shell.

A sea turtle's flippers are powerful and allow them to swim easily. They are clumsy on land.

Unlike other kinds of turtles, sea turtles cannot tuck their head and **limbs** into their shell.

Habitat

Sea turtles are often found in bays, estuaries, and areas along the coast. Some may go farther out to sea.

Some sea turtles prefer shallow, muddy water where they can find lots of food to eat.

Range

Sea turtles are found in the Indian, Atlantic, and Pacific oceans.

They need to be in warm water. If it gets too cold, sea turtles can become stunned.

Diet

Most sea turtles are **omnivores**. They eat both meat and plants.

Their diet is made up of jellyfish, clams, sponges, grasses, and algae. They also eat **crustaceans** like crabs, shrimp, and krill.

Sea turtles often look for food on the ocean floor. They can find plants and **crustaceans** there.

A sea turtle's jaw plays an important role in its diet. Some have an angled jaw that helps them get food from narrow spaces.

Other sea turtles have strong jaws that are designed to help them crush and grind their food.

Some sea turtles start out eating only meat, then eat only plants as they get older.

Communication

Sea turtles use sound and movement to communicate with each other.

Researchers believe that sea turtles are able to make a low-pitched call. They use it to find other sea turtles and when they are travelling together.

Some sea turtles touch or make certain movements to communicate.

Movement

Sea turtles are very slow on land. Their flippers are better in the water than they are on land.

Their heartbeat slows down when they are diving. This allows them to dive deeply and stay under the water for hours at a time.

Sea turtles need to return to the surface to breathe. Some can stay underwater for about seven hours.

Young Sea Turtles

Sea turtles must return to land to lay eggs. They find a spot on a beach at night and dig a hole.

Sea turtles lay between 50 and 200 eggs, then cover their nest with sand. The eggs hatch about two months later.

The hatchlings, or young turtles, make their way to the water on their own.

Sea Turtle Life

Most sea turtles are **solitary**. They spend most of their time alone. Some sea turtles join in large groups when they are going long distances.

Sea turtles are usually **diurnal**. They are most active during the day. The main exception is when they lay eggs.

Mother sea turtles come ashore to lay their eggs at night. It helps her to stay safe from predators.

Lifespan

Most sea turtles have very long lives. It can be hard to know exactly how long because they can be hard to find and study in the wild.

Many researchers believe that most sea turtles live about fifty years in the wild.

Some sea turtles live over 100 years. One was believed to have lived 175 years.

Population

Researchers count sea turtle nesting sites to help them **estimate** populations.

Some researchers believe that sea turtle populations have been growing. Others do not agree. They believe that the populations have been **overestimated**.

Nearly all kinds of sea turtles are **endangered**. There are not many left in the wild.

Sea Turtles in Danger

Sea turtles are facing many threats. One major threat is pollution. When garbage ends up in the ocean, it can hurt or kill animals like sea turtles.

Sea turtle nests are often on beaches that people visit. They can be destroyed if someone walks on them.

Fishing nets are also a threat to sea turtles. When they get tangled in the nets, they can't get to the surface to breathe.

Helping Sea Turtles

In some countries, there are laws to protect sea turtles. It is **illegal** to harm or bother them.

Many beaches have special nets and signs they put up. They prevent sea turtle nests from being destroyed.

Special fishing nets prevent sea turtles from being caught in the net. They keep sea turtles safe.

Many groups are trying to educate people about sea turtles. They hope that people will want to help if they know about the problem.

Glossary

Cold-blooded: an animal whose temperature changes with the surrounding temperature

Crustaceans: animals with hard, jointed shells

Diurnal: animals that are most active during the day

Endangered: at risk of becoming extinct

Estimate: to take a careful guess

Illegal: against the law

Limbs: parts of the body that can move and bend (arms, legs)

Omnivore: an animal that eats both meat and plants

Overestimated: to make an estimate that is too high

Scutes: a hard, bony plate found on some reptiles

Solitary: living alone

About the Author

Victoria Blakemore is a first grade teacher in Southwest Florida with a passion for reading.

You can visit her at

www.elementaryexplorers.com

Also in This Series

Also in This Series